Native American Lives

# Charles Albert Bender

## National Baseball Hall of Fame Pitcher

Written by Kade Ferris

Illustrated by Tashia Hart

**Minnesota Humanities Center**

Lerner Publications ◆ Minneapolis

GENEROUSLY SUPPORTED BY

This book has been supported by the Minnesota Humanities Center, generously funded through the Shakopee Mdewakanton Sioux Community (SMSC) through its Understand Native Minnesota campaign, also funded in part by the Arts and Cultural Heritage Fund that was created with the vote of the people of Minnesota on November 4, 2008, and the National Endowment for the Humanities.



Lerner Publications Company
An imprint of Lerner Publishing Group, Inc.
241 First Avenue North
Minneapolis, MN 55401 USA

For reading levels and more information, look up this title at www.lernerbooks.com.

Illustration credits: Tashia Hart
Image credits: Library of Congress, back cover, pp. 6, 23; Robert G. Beaulieu/Minnesota Historical Society, p. 12; Cumberland County Historical Society, Carlisle, PA, p. 18; The Philadelphia Press, 10/18/1910 p1, via National Archives, p. 24; Sporting News via Getty Images, p. 43. Background pattern: Anastasiia Gevko/Shutterstock.

Main body text set in Noto Serif. Typeface provided by Google Open Source.

**Library of Congress Cataloging-in-Publication Data**

Names: Ferris, Kade, author. | Hart, Tashia, illustrator.
Title: Charles Albert Bender : National Baseball Hall of Fame pitcher / Written by Kade Ferris ; Illustrated by Tashia Hart.
Description: Minneapolis, MN : Lerner Publications, [2026] | Series: Native American lives | Includes bibliographical references and index. | Audience: Ages 9–14 | Audience: Grades 4–6 | Summary: "National Baseball Hall of Fame's Charles Albert Bender had a great career as a pro baseball pitcher. Readers will learn all about Bender's life, including his childhood and pro career playing and coaching baseball"— Provided by publisher.
Identifiers: LCCN 2024045557 (print) | LCCN 2024045558 (ebook) | ISBN 9798765671795 (paperback) | ISBN 9798765679937 (epub)
Subjects: LCSH: Bender, Charles Albert, 1884–1954—Juvenile literature. | Indian baseball players—Biography—Juvenile literature. | Pitchers—United States—Biography—Juvenile literature. | Baseball players—United States—History—Juvenile literature. | Baseball—United States—History—Juvenile literature. | National Baseball Hall of Fame and Museum—Juvenile literature.
Classification: LCC GV865.B36 F47 2026 (print) | LCC GV865.B36 (ebook) | DDC 796.357092 [B]—dc23/eng/20241121

LC record available at https://lccn.loc.gov/2024045557
LC ebook record available at https://lccn.loc.gov/2024045558

Manufactured in the United States of America
1-1012016-54281-3/17/2025

# Table of Contents

# Introduction

Storytelling, a traditional tool of many Indigenous peoples, is alive and well among Native Americans of many nations. The authors, illustrators, and editors of this series, who are all Dakota or Ojibwe, continue their cultural traditions in creating these books and telling stories of leaders, athletes, teachers, and artists.

This series of books is by, for, and about Dakota and Anishinaabe (Ojibwe) and other Indigenous peoples. In portraying our histories, knowledge ways, culture keepers, and beloved figures, these biographies help Dakota, Anishinaabe, and other Native American children imagine their own potential for full futures.

We prefer to be called by our tribal names (Dakota, Ojibwe, or Anishinaabe) or "Native American" or "Indigenous." We use "Indian" in

numerous contexts today, such as the "National Museum of the American Indian." In this series, you will see the use of the term "Indian" in historical context, and not as a derogatory name.

We hope readers will consider how the facts of social barriers based on race, culture, education, and class are part of the life stories in these books. History, especially the impacts of treaties, underlies these stories as well. The legacy of forced education in the English language by government and religious schools, poverty, and the disruption of family life are also themes. The Indigenous peoples featured in these narratives overcame such circumstances. Natural talent in art and sports, leadership skills, and Native American cultural strengths are also themes of their stories.

This series includes stories of historical figures who lived, worked, and broke barriers a hundred years ago, as well as the ongoing accomplishments of exceptional Ojibwe and Dakota people who became leaders, athletes, teachers, and artists, and whose life stories are meaningful today. Our hope is that you see yourselves in the extraordinary lives presented in these books.

—Gwen N. Westerman and Heid E. Erdrich,
series editors, May 2024

Charles Albert Bender

**Mandowescence**

## CHAPTER 1

# FROM THE FORESTS TO THE FIELDS

How many times have you given something your best effort? We all want to win, but is winning all there is? Sometimes, just knowing you've given your best effort, even if you lose, is enough. Hard work and dedication matter more than simply winning. This idea defined the life of Charles Albert Bender.

Charles was born in 1884 along a small lake near Brainerd, Minnesota. He was the fourth of eleven children. His father, Albertus, was a German American who came to Minnesota to be a lumberjack. His mother, Mary Razor, was from the Mississippi

Band of Ojibwe, who lived at the headwaters of the Mississippi River.

Mr. and Mrs. Bender both had to work long hours to take care of their large family. Along with the other lumberjacks, Mr. Bender cut wood all day long. Mrs. Bender worked as a cook for the men. Even though life was a challenge, they were able to earn a living for a few years until all the trees were cut down. Once all the trees were gone, the family moved west to the White Earth Reservation, looking for new opportunities.

At White Earth, the Benders hoped to start a farm. They were able to get land to homestead, but it was a poor patch that was swampy, hilly, and full of rocks. Most of the good land had already been taken by other tribal members and white settlers. The Benders had a hard time starting out and struggled to pay for food, clothes, and other things children need.

Farming was a family job. Everyone had to do their part. Charles's job was to pick up rocks in front of the plow to make planting easier. He walked along the plow's path and picked up the stones. Then he would throw them out of the field so they wouldn't hurt the plow or the horses that pulled it. It was hard work, but after a while, Charles had a very strong arm.

He could hit almost everything he wanted when throwing rocks.

Everyone helped out the best they could, but the Benders still struggled to feed their family. They decided that their oldest children should go to school, where they could get at least one meal a day. At that time, the schools on the White Earth Reservation were very crowded. In 1891, they sent their children to an off-reservation boarding school in Pennsylvania, where they could live and learn with other Native and white children whose parents could not care for them. Eight-year-old Charles, his brother John, and his sister Anna were put on a train headed east. They rode for several days and arrived at the Lincoln Institute near Philadelphia.

## Chapter 2

# Grade School Days

The Lincoln Institute, like most Indian boarding schools, wanted to make Native American children adapt to white society. The hope was that taking Native children from their families would cause the children to leave their traditional ways behind. Native children could learn the English language, work trade jobs for a living, and learn how to be more like white people.

Charles soon found that life at the school was hard. He and the other students had to wake up early in the morning, make their beds, and dress in uniforms. Before breakfast, they were made to march in formation and do exercises. Then they lined up to say the Pledge of Allegiance to the American flag.

Homes on the White Earth Reservation in 1880

After breakfast, students learned subjects such as English and math, and then they did chores at the school's farm. They also milked cows and planted and harvested crops.

Like most students, some of whom were orphans, Charles and his brother and sister were not allowed to go home. If they were lucky, some students had a few visits from family. But because his family was poor, Charles and his siblings went many years without seeing their parents. Finally, when he was twelve, Charles returned home to his family at White Earth. He had spent five years at the Lincoln Institute.

Charles was happy to see his family, but the work was hard. Thirteen people lived in their small home, and Charles was miserable. One day, he and his brother John went to get water for the house. It was a long walk, and their father got angry when they took so long. Their father kicked Charles, who fell down and spilled the water. His father demanded they go back to get more, which made Charles angry. He and his brother decided to run away from home to a relative's farm. When they got there, they refused to go home.

Not too long after that, a teacher came to White Earth to recruit students for a new school. He met Charles and John and told them they could attend if they wanted to go. This opportunity made Charles very happy. He had enjoyed school when he was at the Lincoln Institute. He liked learning and thought it would be better than having to live in his crowded home. Charles accepted the offer. On September 5, 1896, he was back on a train to Pennsylvania and on his way to the Carlisle Indian Industrial School.

## Chapter 3

# Carlisle School

When Charles and his brother arrived at Carlisle, the school staff made them pose for a "before" picture. Then they were given a bath, a haircut, and a uniform and had to stand for an "after" picture. All new students were photographed this way. The school wanted photos to show how it changed students from what non-Native people considered "savage," or wild and dangerous, to "civilized," or looking and behaving like white people.

Students were not allowed to speak their Native languages and used only English at Carlisle. The school made students who had only Native American names choose a new English name from a chalkboard. Charles and his brother already had

English names because their father was white. Teachers also made sure the students did not socialize with other students from their home area, even if they were siblings.

Carlisle was a vocational training school, which meant the students held jobs as part of their education. Staff at Carlisle reminded the students that their land was gone, and they could no longer hunt and fish for a living. Students started the day very early, and they had to work hard. They spent half of each day studying reading, writing, and math. The rest of the day they learned a trade.

Some boys learned to become farmers. They learned how to choose and plant crops, drive tractors, fix equipment, and milk cows. Other students learned how to make boots and shoes that were sold to the nearby military

base. Other trades included carpentry, plumbing, tailoring, and printing. Learning a trade was seen as a way to "civilize" the students and make them future productive citizens.

Most of the girls at Carlisle were not taught job skills. Instead, they were taught to be good wives and mothers or servants. They learned how to sew, make dresses, do laundry, cook, and take care of children. Some girls learned how to be nurses. Their teachers told them that they needed these skills so they could support their families.

As students approached graduation, the school sent them to live with a white family for one year. During that year, students would attend school and work in their given trade. This practice was called an "outing." The staff at Carlisle hoped that some of the students would also learn to model the behaviors of their host families and become what they believed were successful American citizens.

While the Carlisle School was very strict, it did offer some fun for the students. Students could participate in music, speech, journalism, arts and crafts, and sports. It was sports that made Carlisle famous and what helped turn Charles Bender into a legend.

Athletics were very popular at Carlisle. The school's leaders thought sports were a great way to help "civilize" the student athletes. Sports also kept the students busy and were a welcomed social activity. Students could play games with their friends and enjoy time away from classes and their trades.

Football, basketball, and baseball were very popular. Football was the most popular because it was coached by the legendary Glenn "Pop" Warner. During his time at Carlisle, Warner coached many students who excelled at their given sports. One was Jim Thorpe, from the Sac and Fox Nation, who was a two-time All-American in football under Pop Warner. Thorpe also won gold medals in the decathlon and pentathlon—track-and-field events—in the 1912 Olympics.

Even though he would become a legendary athlete himself, Charles was not immediately interested in sports at Carlisle. The first two years at school, he focused on his classwork and learned his trade as a watchmaker.

One day, Charles was hanging around the gym with his friends. They needed someone to pitch to them for practice, so Charles decided to give a

Bender (*top row, sixth from left*) and other students of the 1902 Carlisle Indian School graduating class

few throws. Having developed a strong arm from throwing rocks in the fields back in White Earth, he was a natural. His pitches zoomed! His natural talent immediately caught the eye of Coach Warner, who quickly asked him to join the varsity baseball team.

Starting in 1898, Charles starred on the team as a pitcher and second baseman. He helped his team win games against white high schools and colleges across Pennsylvania. Charles was a successful player and a good student. He kept up with his studies and was a model for other students through his hard work and dedication.

As his graduation day approached in 1901, Charles was faced with a decision. He was trained to go directly to work as a watchmaker, but he thought he might want to go to college instead. Nearby was Dickinson College, which offered a special opportunity. They had a pre-college program for Native American students.

Charles loved school and attended classes at Dickinson College for one year. He enjoyed it, but there wasn't an opportunity to play baseball there.

## Chapter 4
# An Up-and-Coming Prospect

During the summer of 1902, Bender got his first taste of competitive baseball with the semipro Harrisburg Athletic Club. He pitched and played in the field and enjoyed the challenge of playing against good players from around the country. The highlight of that season was an exhibition game against the Chicago Cubs, a pro team. Bender's coach picked him to pitch against the Cubs. Though he did his best against the pro stars, he and his team lost the game.

A scout from the Philadelphia Athletics attended the game to watch the Cubs in action. He immediately reported to the Athletics' manager, Connie Mack, that there was an amazing talent pitching for Harrisburg. Mack went to watch Bender play and was impressed. Mack decided on the spot to offer him a contract to pitch professionally for them. Bender signed for $1,800 (about $50,000 today).

At 19, Bender became a rookie with the Athletics. A kid just out of high school could be scared by the pressure of pro sports, but Bender was a warrior. In his very first game, he was called in when the starting pitcher floundered. Bender pitched six innings and won the game over the legendary pitcher Cy Young of the Boston Americans (later known as the Red Sox). Impressed with his calm and collected skill, Coach

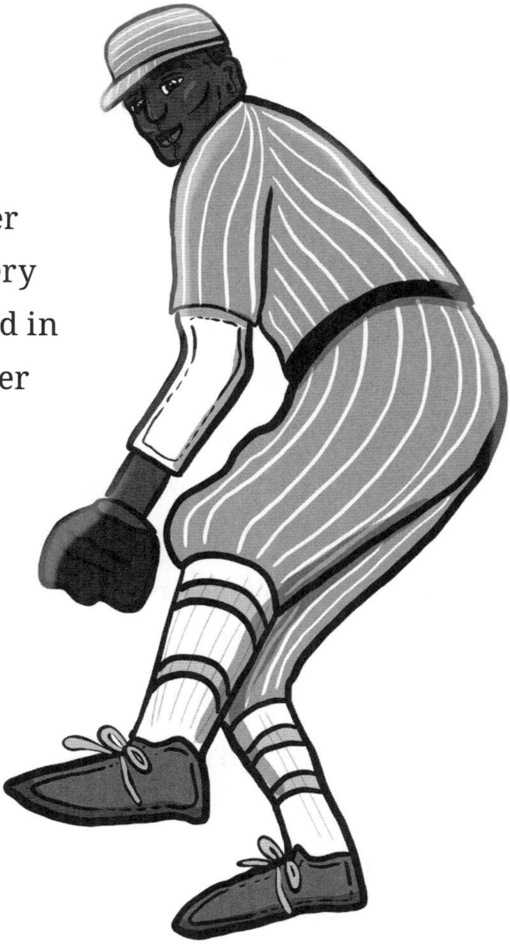

Mack had Bender start the next game. Bender went toe to toe with future Hall of Fame pitcher Clark Griffith of the New York Highlanders. Bender won the game with a shutout!

While he had ups and downs throughout the 1903 season, Bender started in 33 games and completed 29 of them. He won 17 games and allowed just over three runs a game. His team finished second in the league, and many considered Bender to have had one of the best rookie seasons in pro baseball.

Heading into the 1904 season, expectations were high for the Athletics. They were even higher for Bender, the flashy, young pitching sensation. He had been impressive in a few of his starts, but overall, he struggled during the 1904 season. The team finished in fifth place. Bender won 10 games and lost 11, but Coach Mack thought he had gained good experience and encouraged him to practice harder. Bender took the advice, put his poor season behind him, and looked forward to the next season.

Bender improved his pitches in 1905. He pitched about seven innings in each game he started, and he won 18 games out of 23 starts that year. Very reliable when asked to fill in as a reliever, Bender finished 12 games for other pitchers. The Athletics dominated that season and scored almost 100 more runs than the year before.

Finishing their league in first place put the Athletics in the 1905 World Series. Their opponent was the New York Giants, who had won 105 games. The Giants were favored to win the series easily. During Game 1, the Giants beat the Athletics with a shutout by the legendary pitcher Christy Mathewson. Bender was named to start Game 2 of the series.

Everyone figured the young Native American pitcher would lose. Coach Mack gave his team a

Bender in his Philadelphia Athletics uniform in 1909

pep talk, then took Bender to the side. He said that he believed in Bender and that all he needed to do was relax and do his best. Bender didn't want to disappoint his team or his coach. Over the first two innings, he held steady. Then, in the third inning, the

Press

Don't overlook the biggest game of all—the race for "Press" free libraries. See the plan on page 10.

RNING, OCTOBER 18, 1910. ONE CENT.

Scene in Bleachers

ATHLETICS WIN FIRST GAME IN WORLD'S SERIES

Indian Bender's Wonderful Pitching and Baker's Hitting Give Mackmen 4 to 1 Victory.

TY COBB DESCRIBES STRUGGLE

Champion Batsmen of World Tells How Great Contest Was Won—Praises Ira Thomas.

BY "TY" COBB

Champion Batsman of the World.
Copyright, 1910, The Press Company.
"The Philadelphia Press."

Chief Bender's wonderful pitching and the offensive work of Frank Baker won for the Athletics yesterday over the Chicago Cubs in the opening game of the World's series of 1910. It was a phenomenal game and when it is considered that no Chicago player passed first base in eight innings, Bender's feat can be recorded as one of the greatest games ever known in a big series.

That Bender was able to go through eight innings without a man getting past first and without a Cub having been left on the paths, not only illustrates the remarkable nerve, speed and control which the Indian twirler exhibited, but it also shows that the Athletics played jam-up ball. But for two unfortunate and possibly excusable errors in the ninth inning I think the Chief would have not only scored a shut-out, but would have finished the game with a record which would have made the baseball statisticians search their books to discover when it had been equalled.

It sure was a grand game. And the Athletics deserved to win it. Bender outpitched Overall and McIntire and the Mackmen played better both offensively and defensively. And the snappy work of Thomas behind the plate was a big asset.

An analysis of yesterday's game makes it even more evident that it was Bender and Baker who were the big factors in winning it. The Chief allowed only three hits, one in the first inning and two in ninth. He struck out eight Cubs and issued only two passes. Which goes to show just how effective the big Indian was and why the Cubs did not do anything offensively until the final period.

An article about Bender playing in the 1910 World Series

Athletics scored a run. That was all Bender needed. He allowed only four hits and struck out nine batters.

That win was the only win the Athletics would get in the World Series that year. Bender pitched again in Game 7, but they lost the series five games to one. The press began to call Bender "Chief" because he was Native American. A reporter with *The Sporting News* asked about his Ojibwe heritage. Bender was proud of who he was and where he came from, but he told the reporter, "I do not want my name to be presented to the public as an Indian, but as a pitcher." Even so, the nickname Chief stuck with him his whole life.

## Chapter 5

# Inventing the Slider

Bender decided to learn from the loss of the 1905 World Series. Having faced Mathewson twice, Bender wanted to improve his own game. He worked hard over the offseason and developed more control over his pitches. He also learned how to throw different pitches that would work better against opposing batters.

As a fast learner, Bender learned to throw a fadeaway screwball. It looked like a straight pitch, but the ball moved toward the batter to fool them. After mastering this pitch, Bender experimented with improving different techniques and variations. Knowing that some batters could focus on a slow curveball, Bender created a new pitch. It was a sharp, fast-breaking curveball that he called a "slider." The slider pitch was a curveball with a new twist. By throwing hard to make it look like a regular fastball, and by gripping the ball differently, Bender could make it "slide" at the end to move away from the batter. Nobody had ever thought to throw the ball like this before!

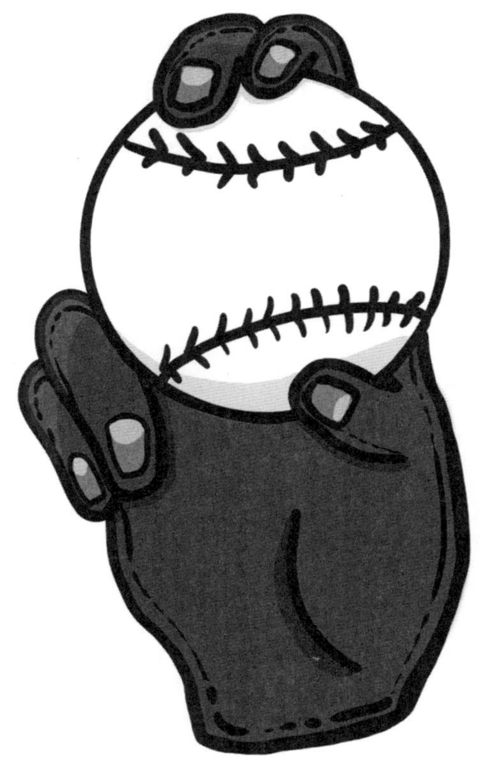

Later in life, when asked how he created the slider, Bender mentioned that he used to experiment as a pitcher. He pitched overhand and sidearm, fast curves, and high and inside fastballs. He also had an underhand fadeaway pitch with his hand almost down to the level of his knees. His ability to throw so many different pitches made it difficult for batters to hit against him.

Armed with his new pitches and his World Series experience, Bender entered the 1906 season with high hopes. He did his best and lowered the number of runs he allowed in games to about two and a half per game. Unfortunately, the rest of the team's performance slipped, and the Athletics finished in fourth place. But Bender had earned a place as one of the pitching aces of the Athletics for years to come.

## Chapter 6

# Facing Racism Despite Achievement

In 1907, the Athletics improved and finished second place in their division. They put on an impressive run but finished just behind the Detroit Tigers. Bender won 16 games that season. He lowered his runs allowed per game to almost two and allowed less than one hit per inning.

Even though his fame was spreading on the baseball diamond, he still faced racism as a Native American. During a series in Washington, DC, Bender had the afternoon off. He decided to look around the city. He spent the day window-shopping and looking at the city's great monuments and the

White House. Deciding he needed a cool drink, Bender went into a malt and soda shop. He asked the owner for a lemon seltzer. Instead of serving him his drink, the man yelled at Bender to get out and said he wasn't allowed there.

Bender was surprised. He was taught at the Carlisle School that an educated Native American was as good as a white man. He repeated his order. The man ignored his request and called for help from another worker. Together, they grabbed Bender and threw him out of the shop and onto the ground. While Bender was used to people making racist war whoops at games, calling him "Chief," and making racist cartoons about him in the press, this was the first time he faced physically violent racism.

Philadelphia was disappointed with the results of the 1908 season. The Athletics lost 85 games and had only 68 wins. Bender was injured much of the year and pitched in only 18 games. He won nine of his games and lowered his earned runs to under two per game, but he didn't make a very impressive impact on the field.

The next year was a bounce-back year for Bender and the Athletics. The team improved so much that they nearly took first place in their division. Bender

also improved. He won 18 games and allowed the seventh-lowest number of runs scored. He had recovered from his injuries and pitched 250 innings over 34 games. His reliability was rewarded as he was moved up to be the number two pitcher in the Athletics rotation that year.

## Chapter 7

# The 1910 World Series

The 1910 season was a magical season for the Athletics. Bender started the season hot and won 14 straight games. He even threw a no-hitter. His 25 wins that year were the fourth best in the league, and his earned run average was fifth best. The Athletics swept their way to 102 wins and were 14 and a half games ahead of the second-place team.

In the World Series that year, Coach Mack picked Bender to start the first game against the Cubs. This was an incredible honor. Bender was nervous, but he was confident in his skills. The game started with a bang. The Athletics scored two runs in the second inning and another in the third. That was all Bender needed to calm his nerves. He held the Cubs to only three hits the entire game. Victory was assured, and Bender allowed only one unearned run in the ninth inning.

The Athletics won the next two games easily. In the fourth game, Bender had the chance to close out the series if he won. He pitched a great game. The Athletics were ahead 3–2 in the bottom of the ninth inning. Bender was only three outs away from winning the World Series for his team. Then the Cubs tied the game and scored again in the 10th inning to win the game. Fortunately, the Athletics won the next game—and they won the World Series.

Losing that one game to the Cubs was devastating for Bender, but his teammates rallied around him. Coach Mack congratulated him for his fine pitching performance and asked Bender how much he owed on his house. Bender replied that it wasn't his business. Coach Mack asked again, and Bender finally told him. To Bender's surprise, Coach Mack offered him a raise in salary equal to what he owed on the house, so he could pay it off.

## Chapter 8

# The King of the Dynasty

Expectations were high heading into the 1911 season. Coach Mack kept his core players happy in the offseason with increased salaries. When spring training rolled around, the team was excited for the new season, and everyone was ready to win it all again—especially Bender.

The Athletics started off hot and never looked back. They led the league all season long. Bender himself was confident, and it showed. He pitched in 34 games that year. He started in 25, won 17, and lost only five! It was by far his best season. Everyone was impressed by his skill and poise. He was becoming known more for his baseball skills and less because people were curious about a Native

American pitcher in Major League Baseball (MLB).

In the first game of the 1911 World Series against the New York Giants, Bender lost a close game to Mathewson. The Athletics won the next two games and took the lead in the series. In Game 4, Bender allowed only two runs and won the game for the Athletics. Things looked up for them, but they lost the next game in a close battle.

Hoping to close out the series in Game 6, Coach Mack looked at his choices. He knew Bender had pitched only two days before and might still be tired. But he was sure Bender could get the job done. He was right. Bender pitched a complete game and sealed it. His pitching at the World Series was hailed as one of the most impressive feats in baseball. He had struck out 20 batters in 26 innings and only allowed one earned run average in the three games he pitched.

The next year was a bit of a letdown. The Athletics struggled to third place in their division, and Bender was injured for part of the season. When he did pitch, he had a few problems. While he won 13 games that year, he lost eight, and his earned run average was nearly three runs per game. He pitched only 171 innings over the entire season in 1912.

During the offseason, Bender worked hard to be

in top shape for the 1913 season. He came into spring looking forward to helping his team improve. He didn't disappoint. That summer, Bender pitched in 48 games—the most on the team. As a relief pitcher, Bender appeared in 24 games and saved 13 of them. Overall, he accounted for 34 of his team's 95 wins. The Athletics easily cruised to first place and were matched against the New York Giants again in the 1913 World Series. Coach Mack knew who he could rely on. He started Bender in Games 1 and 4. Bender won both games by close margins and completed both. The team easily cruised to the series victory in five games.

Many reporters and fans were calling the Athletics a dynasty. They had won three World Series in the past four years. Coming into 1914, the Athletics were favorites to win it all again. Although he was injured for part of the year, Bender performed in near-perfect fashion. He won 17 games and lost only three. His earned run average was near two runs a game, and he struck out twice as many players as he walked that year. The Athletics again took first place and were favored to win against the Boston Braves in the World Series, but they were swept in four games. Bender was beaten soundly in Game 1 of the series. It was the worst performance of his career.

## Chapter 9

# Jumping the Fence

Despite the World Series loss, Bender was proud of the winning record he had helped the Athletics achieve. After the 1914 season, he asked Coach Mack for a pay raise to match his hard work. His request was ignored, and Bender was very disappointed. He felt that he had proved his worth to the team during his career.

In 1915, a new competing baseball league formed. The Federal League offered baseball stars more money to play for their teams. Bender was a hot commodity, and the Baltimore Terrapins offered him $8,000 (about $200,000 today). It was much more than he made with the Athletics, so he accepted. While the grass looked greener on the other side, he found out it wasn't the same.

Bender had played for a supportive coach his entire career, and his new team was not player-friendly. The talent in the new league was different and so were the fans and stadiums. At 31 years old, he knew that a lifetime of hard throwing was taking a toll on his arm. He won only four games for the Terrapins and lost 16. His earned run average was almost four runs per game.

In 1916, Bender accepted a contract from the Philadelphia Phillies. He was happy to return to his adopted hometown. He improved slightly over his disappointing previous season. He won seven games and lost seven games. His earned run average remained near four runs per game, and he pitched only 122 innings that season. The Phillies finished dead last.

The next year was equally bad for Bender. Although both he and the team improved, his injuries limited him to only 113 innings that year. He won eight games, lost two, and lowered his earned run average to less than two runs per game, but he considered the season a failure. The Phillies released Bender, and he retired at the end of 1917. He hoped to get back on the Athletics, but Coach Mack didn't extend him an offer.

## Chapter 10

# Life After the Pros

With his baseball career over, Bender worked at the Philadelphia shipyards in 1918 as World War I (1914–1918) was in its final days. He decided it was his duty to contribute to the war effort and to support his wife, Marie. When the war ended, Bender got right back into baseball. He was hired to manage the Richmond Colts, a minor league team in Virginia. In addition to coaching duties, he occasionally pitched for the Colts.

As a former MLB star, Bender dominated at the minor league level. In 1919, he won 29 games, lost two, and had an earned run average just above one run per game. His team won the league. His impressive performance piqued the interest of some MLB teams.

However, Bender was making as much money as a manager in the minors as he would as a player in the majors.

During the 1920 and 1921 seasons, Bender was a player and manager for the New Haven Indians. The team was excited to have Bender as their coach. As a pitcher, Bender won 25 games in 1920 and 14 games in 1921. His team took first place in 1920 and fourth in 1921. After New Haven, Bender played and coached for the Reading Aces (1922), the Baltimore Orioles (1923), the New Haven Profs (1923), and the Johnstown Johnnies (1924).

In 1925, Bender's former teammate Eddie Collins hired him to be an assistant coach for the Chicago White Sox. Bender was able to share his experience with some of the young players, and he got one last taste of big-league ball. Collins talked Bender into pitching one last major league game. Bender dug deep into his bag of tricks, but age had caught up to him at last. He allowed two runs in one inning of work. After that, he hung up his cleats and retired from playing for good.

## Chapter 11

# Retirement

During the 1930s, Bender opened a sporting goods store in Philadelphia, and he occasionally worked as a coach and baseball consultant. Even as he got older, Bender's baseball knowledge was still sought after by many MLB teams. The Chicago White Sox, New York Yankees, and New York Giants hired him as a pitching coach and as a scout to help them find new pitchers. When Bender was 61 years old, his old Athletics team hired him to pitch batting practice and to mentor their upcoming pitchers. Bender was always ready to share his wisdom and to help young players grow.

In retirement, Bender also learned to enjoy things outside of baseball. He enjoyed trapshooting and loved to hunt and fish. He also became a very good golfer and learned to play pool like a professional. By far, Bender's favorite hobbies were gardening and painting oil landscapes of the beautiful world around him. He enjoyed the beauty of the natural world that he had loved since his childhood in Minnesota.

In 1953, when Bender was 71 years old, he joined the National Baseball Hall of Fame. He lived long enough to enjoy recognition as one of baseball's greatest pitchers. He was the first Minnesotan to be elected to the Hall of Fame. Over his career, Bender

Bender in 1950

won 212 regular season games and six World Series games. He won more than 62 percent of the games he pitched in, and his career earned run average was an amazing 2.46!

The life of Charles Bender is an amazing example of how you can overcome the curveballs that life throws at you by working hard, honing your skills, and giving it everything you have. Bender started life on the shores of a small lake, grew up in poverty on the reservation, and endured racism. He never let any of that get him down or define him.

# Charles Bender Career Statistics

| Year | Age | Team | Wins | Lost | Saves | ERA | BB | SO |
|---|---|---|---|---|---|---|---|---|
| **1903** | 19 | PHA | 17 | 14 | 0 | 3.07 | 65 | 127 |
| **1904** | 20 | PHA | 10 | 11 | 0 | 2.87 | 59 | 149 |
| **1905** | 21 | PHA | 18 | 11 | 0 | 2.83 | 90 | 142 |
| **1906** | 22 | PHA | 15 | 10 | 3 | 2.53 | 48 | 159 |
| **1907** | 23 | PHA | 16 | 8 | 3 | 2.05 | 34 | 112 |
| **1908** | 24 | PHA | 8 | 9 | 1 | 1.75 | 21 | 85 |
| **1909** | 25 | PHA | 18 | 8 | 1 | 1.66 | 45 | 161 |
| **1910** | 26 | PHA | 23 | 5 | 0 | 1.58 | 47 | 155 |
| **1911** | 27 | PHA | 17 | 5 | 3 | 2.16 | 58 | 114 |
| **1912** | 28 | PHA | 13 | 8 | 2 | 2.74 | 33 | 90 |
| **1913** | 29 | PHA | 21 | 10 | 13 | 2.21 | 59 | 135 |
| **1914** | 30 | PHA | 17 | 3 | 2 | 2.26 | 55 | 107 |
| **1915** | 31 | BAL | 4 | 16 | 1 | 3.99 | 37 | 89 |
| **1916** | 32 | PHI | 7 | 7 | 3 | 3.74 | 34 | 43 |
| **1917** | 33 | PHI | 8 | 2 | 2 | 1.67 | 26 | 43 |
| **1925** | 41 | CHW | 0 | 0 | 0 | 18 | 1 | 0 |
| **16 yrs.** | | | **212** | **127** | **34** | **2.46** | **712** | **1,711** |

Baseball Stats Terminology

ERA = earned run average

BB = walk (or base on balls)

SO = strikeout

Team Names

PHA = Philadelphia Athletics

BAL = Baltimore Terrapins

PHI = Philadelphia Phillies

CHW = Chicago White Sox

# Historical Context

The Dakota and Ojibwe people have histories as rich and full of struggle as the US or other countries. This timeline presents important events in one place as a reminder that no one human history is more important than another, but history often makes it look that way. This timeline also provides context from the Dakota and Ojibwe histories. You can use it to respond to the book by comparing the timelines of each person featured in this series to the events listed here.

Beyond memory, this place called Mni Sota Makoce, or Minnesota, is where the people became Dakota. They traveled as far north as Hudson's Bay in Canada, as far west as the Rocky Mountains, south to trade with the Pueblos, and to the southeast past the trading city of Cahokia to the southeastern part of what became the United States.

During this same time, Anishinaabeg, the larger group that includes Ojibwe people, lived far to the east of Minnesota, near the Atlantic Ocean. A series of prophecies, or visions of their future, set the Ojibwe off on their five-hundred-year journey to find a new home in "a land where food grows on water" (meaning manoomin, wild rice) along the Great Lakes and eventually in Minnesota.

# Timeline

| | |
|---|---|
| 900–1400 | The Dakota live, as they have always, in what will become Minnesota; ancestors of other Indigenous groups, including the Ojibwe, begin migrating west. |
| 1540–1622 | Spanish and French explorers map the Mississippi River and Dakota village sites and make contact with the Ojibwe at Lake Superior. |
| 1730–1850 | Ojibwe and Dakota fight over Dakota territories; battles end with their peace agreement in 1870, which remains unbroken. |
| 1776–1783 | The American Revolution is fought. |
| 1805 | The Dakota agree to sell land to the US government, but the US government never pays. |
| 1819 | Fort St. Anthony, renamed Fort Snelling in 1825, is built at Bdote (meeting place of rivers in present-day St. Paul, Minnesota). |
| 1825 | The Dakota and Ojibwe lose land in the Prairie du Chien treaty. |
| 1830 | Congress passes the Indian Removal Act, forcing all Native Americans to move west of the Mississippi River. |
| 1837–1850s | Treaties force the Dakota and Ojibwe onto reservations, and they lose hundreds of millions of acres of homeland. |
| 1849–1857 | Minnesota Territory is established, and American settlers encroach on Dakota lands. |

1858 Minnesota becomes a state.

1861–1865 The American Civil War is fought.

1862 War between the Dakota and the US begins in August and ends in September.

1863 The US repeals treaties, and almost all Dakota are removed from Minnesota.

**1879 Colonel Richard Pratt founds the Carlisle Indian School in Pennsylvania.**

1880s The Dakota people begin to return to their communities in Minnesota.

**1884 Charles Albert Bender is born near Brainerd, Minnesota.**

**1902 Charles Albert Bender graduates from the Carlisle Indian School.**

1924 Congress passes the Indian Citizenship Act, granting citizenship to all Native Americans.

**1925 Bender retires from pro baseball.**

**1934 The US government passes the Indian Reorganization Act, which allows tribes to govern themselves.**

**1953** **Bender joins the National Baseball Hall of Fame.** The US makes laws to end the legal status of tribes as nations during the years known as the Termination era.

**1954** **Bender dies in Pennsylvania.**

1956 The Indian Relocation Act passes to move Native Americans off reservations to cities.

1978 The American Indian Religious Freedom Act ends the outlaw of a tribe's religious and cultural practices.

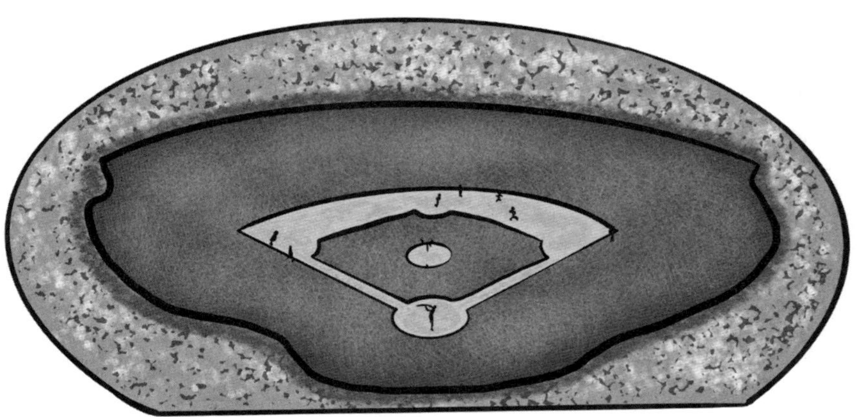

# Glossary

**civilized:** according to racist ways of thinking in Bender's time, to have Native peoples looking and behaving like white people

**consultant:** a person whose job it is to give other people advice on a particular subject such as baseball

**contract:** a written agreement, often between an athlete and a team

**division:** a group of teams within a league

**earned run average:** the average number of earned runs (runs scored without the benefit of an error) per game scored against a pitcher

**homestead:** to settle on land

**reservation:** an area of land held and governed by a Native American tribal nation

**rookie:** a first-year player

**salary:** a fixed amount of money a person earns at a regular time

**savage:** historically, a non-Native person's view that a Native person is wild and dangerous

**scout:** a person whose job it is to look for new baseball talent

**shutout:** when a starting pitcher throws nine innings and doesn't give up a run

**trade:** also known as an occupation or vocation, a job of a specialized craft

# Source Note

25 Tom Swift, “Charles Bender,” Society for American Baseball Research, accessed October 2, 2024, https://sabr.org/bioproj/person/charles-bender/.

# Extend Your Learning

## IDEAS FOR WRITING AND DISCUSSION

- What moment in this story do you think you will most remember? Why?
- Who do you believe was most important to this person's success? Why?
- What do you think were the hardest moments for this person? Why?
- How do you think this person was able to overcome hardship in their life?
- What were the happiest moments in the story of this person's life?
- What moment in the story reminded you of something in your own life?
- Write your own short autobiography, the story of your life so far!

## IDEAS FOR VISUAL PROJECTS

- Draw images for three or four moments that are not illustrated in this book.
- Draw a sketch of this person and include items they liked.
- Find images from American Indian boarding schools from the time this book covers.
- Find historic images to share of activities this book mentions. Are they different now?
- Find historic images to share of the reservations or places this book mentions.

- Make a map of tribal nations near where you live. Where are reservations located? What tribes live there? What else did you learn about these tribal nations?

- Create a bar graph, pie chart, or other infographic on one of these topics:

    1. How many Native Americans live in urban areas near you? Which US cities are home to the largest populations of Native Americans?
    2. How many Native American students are there in your school district? How many tribes are represented?
    3. Explore "Why Treaties Matter" and give a brief report about how treaties formed the reservations and the homelands of Dakota and Ojibwe peoples.

**Resources for Visual Projects**
American Indian Education: Teaching and Learning
https://education.mn.gov/MDE/dse/indian/teach/

Why Treaties Matter
http://treatiesmatter.org/exhibit/

## IDEAS FOR FURTHER LEARNING

The Dakota and Ojibwe people continue to live in Minnesota and are part of all aspects of our society. While English is a shared language, many Dakota and Ojibwe people also study and speak Dakota and Anishinaabemowin, their Indigenous languages.

- Find unfamiliar words in this book, and create a glossary or word list with definitions.

- Create a timeline for this person's life.

- Learn how to count to ten in Dakota or Ojibwe.
- Look up Ojibwe or Dakota words for baseball or other ball games such as lacrosse.
- Learn about Dakota and Ojibwe sports and activities such as powwows.
- Make a list of four common traditions the Ojibwe and Dakota share.

**Resources to Learn More**

Historic Fort Snelling: Educator Resources
https://www.mnhs.org/fortsnelling/learn/educator-resources

Minnesota Historical Society: Beginning Dakota
http://beginningdakota.org

Minnesota Historical Society: Minnesota Territory
http://www.mnhs.org/talesoftheterritory

Minnesota Historical Society: Ojibwe Material Culture
http://www.mnhs.org/ojibwematerialculture

The Ojibwe People's Dictionary
https://ojibwe.lib.umn.edu

# About the Author

**Kade Ferris** was an anthropologist and historian with more than 25 years of experience working with Ojibwe and other tribal communities across the upper Midwest. He received a bachelor's degree in anthropology from the University of North Dakota and a master's degree in anthropology from North Dakota State University. He wrote several books based on his research that focused on the history and culture of the Anishinaabe people. Ferris was of Turtle Mountain Chippewa and Canadian Metis descent and was a proud husband and father of five sons. Known by his Ojibwe name Giniw Wiidokaage (Eagle Helps Him), he passed away on November 4, 2023, and his stories continue to teach everyone.

# About the Illustrator

**Tashia Hart** is an author and illustrator; her works include *Native Love Jams* (2023), *The Good Berry Cookbook: Harvesting and Cooking Wild Rice and Other Wild Foods* (2021), *Gidjie and the Wolves* (2020), and *Girl Unreserved* (2015). She was assistant illustrator for *Gaa-pi-izhiwebak* (2021) and illustrator for *Gidjie and the Wolves* (2020). Her short works include recipes, essays, poetry, and short stories for various publications. In addition to this title, she has also illustrated several of the books in this series. She is a citizen of the Red Lake Nation and resides in Duluth, Minnesota.

# About the Series Editors

**Heid E. Erdrich** is a member of the Ojibwe Nation enrolled at the Turtle Mountain Reservation in North Dakota. She grew up in Wahpeton, North Dakota. She is also German American and Metis from Canada. Erdrich has written several books of poetry and a cookbook focused on Indigenous foods. Along with being Anishinaabe/Ojibwe, Erdrich's extended family includes Dakota, Hidatsa, Somali American, German American, and immigrants from India. She loves the stories of how many kinds of people came to call one place home. Erdrich has lived in Minnesota for many years, raising her kids in Minneapolis, where they went to public schools.

**Gwen N. Westerman** is Dakota from the Sisseton Wahpeton Oyate and a citizen of the Cherokee Nation of Oklahoma. She grew up in Kansas among many different tribal nations. Today, she writes about Dakota history, and writes poetry in English and Dakota. Westerman's ancestors were teachers, leaders, and hard workers who were Dakota, Cherokee, Ojibwe, and Odawa along with a few French and Scottish traders. She lives in Minnesota, where her kids grew up playing ice hockey and soccer.